The Believer's Guide to the

JESUS
GYM

8/13

The Believer's Guide to the

JESUS GYM

Pastor
H. Lionel Edmonds

TATE PUBLISHING
AND ENTERPRISES, LLC

Published by Tate Publishing & Enterprises, LLC
127 E. Trade Center Terrace | Mustang, Oklahoma 73064 USA
1.888.361.9473 | www.tatepublishing.com

Tate Publishing is committed to excellence in the publishing industry. The company reflects the philosophy established by the founders, based on Psalm 68:11,
"The Lord gave the word and great was the company of those who published it."

Book design copyright © 2011 by Tate Publishing, LLC. All rights reserved.
Cover design by Kristen Verser
Interior design by Christina Hicks

Published in the United States of America

ISBN: 978-1-61346-725-1
1. Religion / Christian Life / Personal Growth
2. Religion / Christian Life / General
11.11.10

TABLE OF CONTENTS

CHAPTER ONE

Imagine getting on the bathroom scales one day and not liking what you see. This perhaps may be more fact than fiction for many of us. Your response at this point may determine the destiny and future of your physical life. At this stage of the game, you have two options. You could get upset at the scale and toss it out of the window (not my personal suggestion), or you could decide that it is time to do something about the situation. You might make up your mind to make the effort to shed the pounds and let the true you come shining through.

This book is about those of us on the Christian journey who have gotten on the scales of our religious lives and become dissatisfied with what we have detected. Here we also have a couple of options to consider. We could go into denial and bury our heads in the sand, thus becoming frustrated followers of Jesus; or we could begin the process of inward development of the new creation in Christ. I know that denial is not an option for you, that you desire to let go of the unwanted weight that is wrapped around your spiritual frame. Despite what the scales may indicate, you affirm that eye has not seen the glorious you that is presently covered up. Being in the "Jesus gym" means to begin the steps to shed the weight or, as the Apostle Paul puts it in Hebrews 12:1 (ASV), "lay aside the weight of sin that so easily keeps us down." I like this definition of sin that the apostle is using, for he says that sin is putting off weight.

Where do we go when we want to get into physical shape? We go to a gym or fitness center. Once we join the gym, use the equipment, perhaps hire a trainer, and get on a healthy diet, there's no doubt that the pounds will begin to drop off. Why do we believe in the end results so strongly? Because we realize that although the mirror may reflect something else at the moment, there are some muscles hiding within our physical bodies. These muscles are just waiting for the opportunity to break out, for the fitness program in the gym to eventually manifest the muscle.

This book operates on a similar, albeit higher, principle. You don't have to pray to our heavenly Father to give you some spiritual muscles. In Christ, you already possess what you are praying for. Now it is just about doing what Paul spoke about in another letter to his son in the ministry Timothy, in 1 Timothy 4:7 (ASV), "for bodily exercise is profitable for a little; but godliness is profitable for all things." Paul is saying that godliness, or doing spiritual exercising that reshapes us to become like our Lord Jesus, produces great benefits for us as Christians.

I was at dinner recently with some friends, and I shared with them that I was in the midst of writing this book. I told them that it was a book about spiritual formation. I could tell by their expressions that I was failing to get through to them what the book was about. Then I started using the muscle metaphor. I said that most people acknowledge the fact that they possess a physical muscle, even though they may not exercise it. Likewise everyone has a spiritual muscle, though that spiritual muscle probably is not being exercised either. That is when the light came on within their mental rooms. The moment that I applied this muscle metaphor to our conversation the scales dropped from their eyes, they began to understand what my book is about, and they became excited about it—excited enough, I hope, to go out and buy copies. So no longer think that growth in God is just for a select spiritual few. Entrance into God's fitness center is for whosoever will. As a new person in Christ Jesus, everything you need already is within you. Remember, no gym can bring out of you what is not already within you. But because you possess it, you can display it.

Likewise, the Lord brings out what He has already placed within you. The spiritual formation that you will find in the Jesus gym is to the soul what calisthenics is to the physical body.

Just as there are fundamental exercises that every athlete and physically active person performs to get into, and stay in shape, so also there are essential spiritual exercises within the spiritual formation of the Jesus gym that are meant to make us become a kingdom of royal priests and a chosen generation of powerfully performing disciples of Christ. In the following pages we will take a close look at what spiritual formation is, but for now let me repeat that spiritual formation does for the soul what physical fitness does for the body. It fine-tunes the soul. It develops the spirit. It makes manifest what was once covered up.

During my pastoral ministry of the last three decades, I have had the tremendous blessing to meet and become friends with many wonderful people. It is out of my conversations with these brothers and sisters in Christ that I have come to the conclusion that too many of us live far below our spiritual capacities and divine potential. This is the outcome of harboring the erroneous belief that we do not have the "inner equipment" that promotes a powerful and dynamic spiritual life that overflows into every facet of our social lives. Yet, as soon as one comes to the realization that entering into the Jesus gym is the beginning point for this illumina- tive and love-affirming lifestyle, he or she wonders why the steps had not been taken long ago. There is nothing that can separate us from growth in God once we have tasted and seen the preciousness of the Lord and made the decision not to settle for a taste but to try out the buffet at the kingdom of God banquet. Don't let anyone tell you that it is too late to enter into this Jesus gym. Age is not a factor. Neither is race, creed, or color. Jesus says that anyone may be a member of the Jesus gym.

When I enter my local gym around the corner from my church, the Mount Lebanon Baptist Church in our nation's capital, I immediately see people of all shapes, sizes, and colors. I don't stress out if my shape is not exactly like someone else's in the gym. Neither does a trainer kindly escort me out of the gym for not being in the best of shape or even for being out of shape. Both the trainer and I understand that my physical body can get into a healthier form despite what the scales may say. We both know that there are some exercise machines within the gym that can and will help me meet my goals. Let us go into the Jesus gym with the same expectations.

The Lord operates the same way with His church and His people. In most churches, the usher does not screen guests as they enter the doors of the sanctuary. They don't measure the visitors to see if they "cut the mustard" for being a disciple for the

Lord. No one says, "Hold on a minute, my friend. I regret to inform you that today we are only admitting people who look like they will become strong Christians. You look a little weak at the moment. Try again next Sunday, and have a God-blessed day!" But we know that the Word informs us that entrance into the kingdom of God is open to all.

Yet entrance into His church is the starting point and not the finish. Let's face it; there is no way to experience growth in God by exercising our spiritual muscle for only one hour a week, let alone one hour a month. The kingdom of God should not be inhabited by a bunch of Christian couch potatoes. This book will help you learn how to work out that kingdom muscle between the Sunday shout. Becoming a member of the Jesus gym will transform you from a couch potato child of God into a saint whose spirituality spills over and overflows into his or her family, community, health, and finances.

At times it is kind of funny to sit back and listen to the language that we, as people of God, toss around in our churches. I think much of the terminology that we use is in need of a facelift. Think about it for a minute: how often do we use terms in the church that may sound quite familiar to us who may have grown up inside the church culture but sound strange and bewildering to those folks who have not? Let me talk about myself for a second. I have said these words hundreds of times after the close of one of my sermons and as the way to offer the invitation to discipleship, "The doors of the church are now open." Suddenly it occurred to me that these words probably sound rather peculiar to the visitor. After all, to the visitor's way of thinking, the doors of the church had been unlocked for well over an hour. If they were not open, no one would have been able to come inside for the worship service. Thus, someone who may not be as familiar with some of the language of the church where I serve as senior minister may ask, "What does the preacher mean by that? The only way that I was able to enter the building was due to the fact that the door of the church was open." The need to update what sounds unfamiliar to our ears is also necessary in the area of our growth in God. This is why I call it entering into the Jesus gym. The Jesus gym is all about the ultimate Christian goal of having the life of Christ Jesus fill us and flow through us, resulting in our growing more and more in His likeness. It is updating our definition of growing in the Lord. But instead of me saying all of that, the little phrase, "Jesus gym," metaphorically informs you of exactly what I mean in a more up-to-date way.

Many of the things that we will discover as we enter into the gym are, however, as old as the Bible itself. These timeless truths and divine principles were employed by pioneers of our faith and produced profound and powerful results in their spiritual lives. These exercises still contain tremendous benefit for those of us who decide to use them now.

Thus I will not say anything new, for nothing new can be said. I will attempt, however, to say it in such a way that you will have the desire to put it into practice. No scholarly expertise in scripture will be needed. We will do what the original meaning of the word "educate" implies; we will simply lift up and out of us what already exists within us. When we walk into the physical fitness center, we don't go to the desk and ask for a new set of muscles, even though that does sound pretty nice. What we do, once inside the training center, is to strengthen and tone the muscle that already has been placed within us by God. I think that the physical muscle is, in some mysterious way, representative of the spiritual muscle that the Lord has placed within us. To put it another way, the visible muscle is the manifestation of the spiritual one.

Thinking of growth in God along these lines might change the way we pray. Instead of asking the Lord to give us strength from an outside place, we may now say, "Lord, cultivate in us the spiritual muscle that you have already divinely deposited within us." Knowing that we already possess that for which we are asking is a powerful and blessed new way to approach life. You already possess it. We only need to come to know it and develop it. It will be exciting to wake up each day with the understanding that everything you encounter this day is for the purpose of your for inner development and divine growth.

How to Eat an Elephant

Some of you are saying that this way of life and looking is going to require a big change in your part. Have you ever heard the story of how to eat an elephant? The way to eat an elephant is one bite at a time. We are going to take this thing called spiritual growth one bite at a time, just like when you go to the gym to do some weight lifting and strength training. The novice does not try to lift a two-hundred pound set of weights the first time out. A ten-pound set will do just fine, thank you. One bite at a time. We are not trying to compete with anyone to see who has the better spiritual body. We are just going to let our personal light shine. On my professional ministry level, the day that the Lord showed me this truth and I received it was the day I stopped trying to imitate other ministries and impersonate other pastors. Let go and let God. Enter the Jesus gym.

Let's now take the first steps and enter the Jesus gym to do some looking around. One of the first exercises that we come across in the Jesus gym that countless great men and women of faith have used is the exercise tools called contemplation, solitude, and stillness. Remember that I told you that we should try to do some updating of these terms and practices. So, if these words sound strange for now, don't close the book. I'll bet that before we get too far along, you will discover that you are already instinctively doing what I am placing before you.

I had no idea what a "grande soy latte" was until I walked into a Starbucks one morning and decided to order one. The words that Starbucks used to describe its beverages were strange and unfamiliar to me. Nevertheless, I ordered one, with the assistance of the coffee barrister (a fancy term for coffee maker). Now I'm hooked. I want to get you hooked on developing your spiritual muscle.

The First Bite.

Stillness/Solitude

Let's get back to this thing called silence or solitude. Now we may think that this is some kind of practice meant for people who wander through the desert and are waiting to hear a deep baritone voice crack the clear blue sky. In reality, solitude is the gift that God has given to all of His children to enable them to experience His presence and to hear His voice in the most common and ordinary of places.

When we settle down and become still, we give ourselves the chance to encounter what the author of Genesis was talking about when he said that God made us in His image and likeness. Christ Jesus entered the world to allow those who believe and follow him the opportunity to return to embracing our image as children of God and walking within that divine likeness. Please don't think that your divine image and likeness of God has been forever lost. In Christ, it can always be recovered and embraced. It may be covered up due to the hectic pace of our present conditions, but contemplation is the exercise of uncovering what was once hidden. When we become still, we are coming back home to the Lord.

Do you remember how it feels to finally make it back home after a long and tedious business trip or a supposed "vacation"? Nothing feels as good as to finally make it home. It's as if a weight has been dropped from our shoulders as we plop down on the couch and simply let the presence of being in a relaxed and familiar place to start to sink in. As it sinks deeper and deeper within, the presence of home begins to untie the knots that the airport or the highway twisted within us, and we say to ourselves that it is good to be home. Even so, solitude is a feeling of coming to our true home; it is letting the Lord do His work of untying the knots that the daily grind brings us as we learn to be still in His presence.

Spiritual formation loosens the knots that life's daily grind twists around our hearts and minds. No one wants to walk around tied up in a big knot, yet it is easy to detect the people who are living tangled and knotted lives. As the song says, "It's written all over your face." We do not have to exist in such a way.

Do you remember the story that Jesus told about the prodigal son? One of the lessons of this profound story is what happens when we leave home and what happens when we return. As soon as the prodigal son left home and strayed away from his father, his life began to take a downward spiral until he wound up living inside a pigpen. We could call him "Mr. Piggy." Pretty soon, while living in that pigpen and looking at those pigs from sunrise to sunset, he started acting like a pig by eating what the pigs ate. Frequently, you become what you allow yourself to see and to enter into your mind. A wise man once said, "What you see, man, you will become." In the case of the prodigal son, seeing pigs in a pigpen filled up most of his day and he began to behave like Mr. Piggy. Yet, despite taking up residence in a one-room pig apartment, the divine imprint that God had placed within him could not ultimately be blocked out. He did a little reflection and contemplation in that pigpen, and this period of solitude allowed him to "come to himself" and start the return trip back home to a loving father.

Pastor H. Lionel Edmonds

Every pigpen situation has another side, one that affords us the opportunity to start to see things in a higher way. Solitude is the silent act of starting to see life with a heavenly perception. When we start to cultivate the vision that Jesus has of us and make the investment in that higher point of view, then we are travelling homeward bound to our heavenly Father. We begin to see ourselves as God intended us to be and become what was first gloriously mentioned way back in the book of Genesis where God looked at us and saw His reflection. He placed the heavenly imprint upon us, and no pigpen can replace it. Take a moment right now to sit silently and ponder upon this great verse of scripture, "And God said, let us make humanity in our own image and our own likeness" (Genesis 1:26 ASV). Disconnection from our divine origin does not mean destruction of the love of God that is in Christ Jesus. As we permit the Spirit of His Son to show us how to be still in the Father's presence, what was once disconnected (our sense of being at home in heaven) is restored.

A certain gentleman was trying to turn his television set on, but it failed to come on. He immediately called the cable company to complain about the situation. When the cable representative answered the phone and as the gentleman began to state his complaint, the representative said, "Sir, I am here to help you. First of all, is your television set plugged in?" The gentleman looked down by the outlet and, sure enough, the plug had gotten disconnected from the outlet. After apologizing profusely, he plugged the set into the outlet and the picture appeared on the screen. There was nothing wrong with the set. It just needed to be plugged in. There is nothing wrong with you either. Union with God means to be "plugged in."

I remember feeling plugged in with the Lord for the first time when I was about sixteen or seventeen years old growing up in Fort Wayne, Indiana. I grew up in a Lutheran family. (I know, you're wondering how I became a Baptist minister. That's a story all by itself.) Being brought up in church, however, is not the same as "being in the church" or living in the power of the Spirit of Christ. Thus, like most teenage boys growing up in urban settings, I did things to try to prove my "street credentials."

One night a couple of friends and I decided that we would permanently borrow a stereo system from a house across town. Once we arrived near the house, one of the boys in the group attempted to enter through a side door while another boy went to the front porch of the house as the lookout. As soon as he walked to the front of the house, the owner jumped out waving a pistol at him and warning us not to move an inch. I panicked and took off running. As I started running, I heard what sounded like a cannon going off. It was the gunshots coming from the homeowner, and the bullets had our heads as the targets. Running, heart pounding and scared to death, I suddenly sensed a hand touching my right shoulder and causing me to lean my head to the right of my body. As I leaned to the right while still running and looking around to see whose hand touched me, I heard the sizzling whistle of a bullet brush past my left ear. The complete catalog of my teenager life flashed before my eyes. That's where and when I got plugged into the reality of my Christian profession. It was at that moment that prayer for me became the awareness of the Good Shepherd. This was my entrance into the deeper side of life. I told the Lord that if He would spare me then, I would serve Him. Jesus did, and I have tried to do my best in service to Him for more than three decades.

That's why I'm talking with you now. I am not trying to put a gun to your head to try to force you to accept anything. Yet I know that you, too, have felt the hand of God somewhere along your journey. I know that His voice echoes deep within the corridors of your soul, lingering around the inner edges, muffled most of the time, but never completely snuffed out. Your connection to a deeper and more powerful way of life is Christ is calling you.

I am a huge *Star Trek* fan, although I never became a member of the "Trekkie" club. I loved to hear the opening words of the show as I sat before our Magnavox television set as a child in the living room: "Space … the last frontier …" Of course, Gene Rodenberry, the visionary creator of the show, was referring to outer space. Not too many of us will get to be astronauts and explore the outer regions of the galaxy. I have discovered an "inner space," however, that can give just as much thrill and excitement to you and me as I once had while sitting before that old floor-model Magnavox.

There is an outer world and an inner world. The majority of us have majored in our understanding of the outer world. From the moment we open our eyes in the morning and instantaneously, without thinking, turn on the television set or the radio, we are almost programmed to start the day in total engagement with the external world around us. If we don't start the day with the remote in our hands, flipping and surfing the cable channels, we reach for the computer mouse to see how many messages we have already received. All of this is done before we take one step out of the house in the morning!

I am not saying that we should stop our engagement with the outer world. That is not what being a Christian is all about and is not what spiritual formation promotes. I am pushing us to have balance in our lives by participating in our inner world, the one that the Bible affirms is the place where God dwells. Focusing only on the outer world will result in our getting out of shape. Engaging in the inner world puts us back into our original form, as the Lord fashioned us to be in the first place. In a way, it's like one of my favorite hats.

The women's ministry at the church held a fashion show and asked the men to participate by wearing one of our favorite hats or suits. I volunteered to wear one of my hats for the event, and decided to take it to a store that I knew cleaned and blocked hats. I showed the salesperson my beat-up looking hat and asked him if he could clean and restore its shape. He said, "This is a beautiful hat. There's no need to put it on the hat block machine. It will return to its original form if you just place it in an upright position and let it sit still for a little while." That's what solitude and stillness do for us as well. When our lives get out of shape, stillness can restore us to our original divine design.

Sometimes people approach me after worship service, or even in a business meeting, and ask how a person becomes spiritual. First, I let them know that it is not nearly as difficult as they might imagine it to be. Leading a spiritual life is as natural to the child of God as it is for a fish to swim in the sea. It is what we are created to be. We simply must take the steps to become what God intended us to be all along. It is our divine birthright. We can rest easy in the knowledge that we already possess the thing that we are searching for. Remember, you don't wish that you had a muscle; you know beyond a shadow of a doubt that you do. There should be no doubt either that your spiritual muscle is just as, if not more, real as our physical one. The stillness that we settle into within solitude will certainly manifest the spiritual muscle.

Pastor H. Lionel Edmonds

There are many men and women in the world who we call geniuses and who exhibit an excellence in their particular fields of endeavor that enhances the world that we live in. Individuals in the sciences, the arts, and in politics who habitually flex their intuitive muscle are the kind of people who the great Ralph Waldo Emerson said possessed the necessity of solitude: "They had that necessity of solitude which genius feels...there are metals like potassium and which, to be sure, must be kept under naphtha...Nature protects her work. To the culture of the world, an Archimedes, a Newton is indispensable: so she guards them by aridity. If these had been good fellows, fond of dancing, port, and clubs, we should have had no Theory of the Sphere and no Principia..."[1]

Now I know the preceding may sound a little like you're back in your high school or college introduction to philosophy class; but what I think Emerson means is that solitude and stillness is the warm-up exercise that manifests the inner gift.

Have you ever thought of yourself as a potential genius? I am not just talking about your mental IQ. The kind of genius that I am referring to is that single parent raising his or her child, going to work everyday, maintain the home, making a contribution to the church and community, and feeling good about his or her life. It's that married couple still in love with each other despite whatever may have come their way. Geniuses are those children who find a way to get into college even though no one else in their environment has a word of encouragement for them. Yet in the stillness of their secret prayer lives, they learn how to speak the word of self- encouragement.

If we start to make an effort, we will find that everyone possesses his or her own God-given brand of genius. Each one of us carries deep within that intuitive muscle called spirituality. Each time we enter our inner room—that place that Jesus refers to as our secret closet—we are stepping closer and closer to our God-given gift of genius. There in the mysterious intimacy of the presence of the Lord, a sacred fellowship begins to form and the overflow of divine intuition spills into our lives. The risen Christ is the one who cultivates the gift within as we exercise our solitude. This spiritual spillover and heavenly overflow is what society terms "genius."

Plato comments on the value of cultivating stillness in a world so overridden with confusion: "When the mind returns to itself from the confusion of sense (that is, of cave life) as it does when it reflects, it passes into another region of that which is pure and everlasting, immortal and unchanging … it feels its welfare under its control and at rest from its wanderings, being, in communion with the unchanging … ." The good news is this place of rest where the genius in each of us abides and is much more than a philosophical pursuit, but by the grace and mercy of God our Father and Jesus our Savior, it is our reality as we put on the mind of Christ and practice stillness and solitude. As Apostle Paul tells us, "Let this mind be in you, that was also in Christ Jesus" (Phillipians 2:5, ASV). When we get quiet, we are allowing the Holy Spirit to nurture our minds and begin to practice of perceiving life the way that Jesus intended His follower to see and live it.

The biblical record is overrun with examples of men and women whose spiritual formation exercise routine used solitude and stillness as a core component and, because of it, they were enabled to lead beautiful, godly, and productive lives. We will see that our growth in God through the use of things like stillness is not a respecter of persons and neither does your age come into play. Remember, all you need is a muscle to qualify.

I teach a class on Sunday mornings that I call "God's Golden Children of the Kingdom." This class is especially designed for those of us who have AARP status. It's not that we discriminate against any other age group, and certainly anyone is welcome, but we are just a tee in a playful kind of way by saying that life doesn't really begin until you enter AARP demographics. That, along with the fact that older people just get up earlier than younger people, may be the reason that most of the members in my class are fifty years old and over.

One Sunday during the class I wanted to press home the point that growth in God is not based on age. So I asked the members of the class to raise their hands if they thought that they had a muscle in their bodies. Of course everyone raised a hand. I then said that, despite being "senior citizens," we still know that, as seniors we have a muscle, and we should be just as confident that we have a spiritual muscle. Then we began to look at some "seniors" in sacred scripture and what they were able to accomplish that would put some of today's young people to shame. We put a holy spotlight on the Apostle

John on the Isle of Patmos, on Daniel in the lion's den, on Moses and Caleb in their march to the land of promise. In each of their lives, one can see the demonstration of a dynamic fellowship with the Lord that is centered in solitude and the practice of stillness before His presence. Fellowship with the heavenly Father is the force that breaks the shackles of physical limitations.

The power of stillness can become your victorious response to the storms that life sometimes hurls your way. Recall when Jesus was asleep in the back of a boat during a storm while His disciples panicked with fear. The story reminds me of a plane ride that I was on a number of years ago. The flight got very bumpy as we encountered some unexpected turbulence. A number of the adults on the plane began to look a little anxious, but there was one little child who remained calm, cool, and collected. I overheard one of the passengers remark to the little boy on how brave he was, and the little boy said, "The bumps don't scare me. My daddy is the pilot." I believe that Jesus could sleep in the storm because He knew that His Father was the pilot of that storm-tossed ship at sea. Nevertheless, to demonstrate His love and care, as well as His command over every contrary situation, Jesus showed us how to dismantle a storm. He said, "Peace, be still." That's how you silence a storm. You release a deep and divine inner peace that surpasses all human understanding and quiets every storm. Solitude anchors us in the depths of God's love and launches us out into the deep things within the kingdom of heaven.

The Apostle Paul knew a thing or two about finding inner strength in order to overcome outward struggles. One day he informed some fellow Christians of what the Lord had taught him. "For I have learned in whatever state I am, therein to be content. I know how to be abased, and I know how to abound. I learned the secret on how to be filled and to be hungry, both to abound and to be in want. I can do all things in Christ who strengthen me." Now this was a person who had to deal with a physical condition (probably eye cataracts), and yet was one of the most productive Christians in the history of our faith.

What was the secret of Paul's overcoming? He says that it was "knowledge," an inner knowledge that goes much deeper than simply book knowledge of a subject. I know many people who can read a cookbook, but that does not mean they know how to cook a meal! In fact, the best cooks know intuitively how much of, as well as what, ingredients to put in a soup or a cake. Knowing how to read the notes on a sheet of music does not always translate into possessing the mastery of the musical instrument that will play the notes on the page. The type of knowing that solitude brings equates to an intimacy between the Lord and His child. This knowing weds the head and the heart. The wonderful news is that you don't need to spend an extra dime or travel from conference to conference to find this knowledge. It has been freely given to you through the grace of God in Christ Jesus, our Lord.

One of my favorite writers is Meister Eckhart, the great German mystic, who was a Dominican priest during the fifteenth century. Eckhart perhaps captivates me because of my early childhood years spent within the hallways and classrooms of Zion Lutheran Grade School in my hometown of Fort Wayne, Indiana. (The school had a lot of German flavor. We were served knockwurst and sauerkraut every Wednesday for lunch. That may be the reason that I can't stand either of them now.) Eckhart once said:

"I have declared that there is a power in the soul untouched by time and flesh, flowing from the Spirit, altogether spiritual. In this power is God flowering in all the joy and glory of His actual Self...."[2]

Eckhart loved to talk about the spark in the soul which flows from the indwelling of the Spirit of the Son of God. His words point us to the power that comes from the life that flows from a spiritual stillness. We usually don't think that being still translates to possessing much power. On the contrary, most people look at movement as the expression of power and strength. But I remember my mother having a lot of power over us as children playing in church during the worship service. She would be up front, singing in the choir. She did not have to move an inch but simply stare at my brother, Michael, and me as we jumped around in the pews. That maternal stare in our direction would freeze our mischievous behavior, forcing us to sit still in the sanctuary or suffer the consequences when we returned home.

There is power in the possession of the centered life that moves with such invisible force that it can cause a physical change to happen with just a facial expression. This is the power "untouched by time and flesh" that Eckhart is talking about. It relates back to the knowledge that we spoke of earlier—the knowledge that Paul said we have as children of God. In fact, this knowledge is power, and this power is knowledge. The two cannot be separated. When we wed knowledge and power, what is birthed is a wisdom that descends from on high. This wisdom is ours to walk in, to live from, and to be enraptured by.

Once we begin to live and walk in the wisdom that stillness in Christ brings to us, our lives become much easier. This does not mean that we will never have problems again in our lives, but these problems will be placed in a spiritual perspective and will not be able to get the best of us. Jesus said that in this world we will have troubles but to be of good cheer, because in Christ we have overcome the world.

I know many people who are always on some kind of a search mission, who are constantly looking for companionship and love, for fun and adventure, for peace and joy. It's time for us to stop chasing after things and let these things chase after us! Isn't that what the psalmist David wrote in the Twenty-third Psalm? David affirmed that goodness and mercy will follow us all the days of our lives. To whom is he referring? David is talking about those who have begun to live by the still waters, that is, those whose lives possess an inner calm and spiritual deepness. These are the people who will see the goodness of God track them down. It's the same sentiment that Paul, the tent maker from Tarsus, was expressing when he said that every good and perfect gift comes down to us from our heavenly Father.

As we begin to understand this great biblical truth of solitude and stillness, we will start to see that the only thing that can really affect us in a negative way is whatever we allow to walk into the inner room of our inward houses, take a seat, and put its feet up on the tables of our hearts.

I recall in my first pastorate, a member came into my study complaining about what another member of the congregation had said about her. As we began to talk about the incident, it was revealed that the situation had occurred over twenty years ago! But she was talking to me as if it had just happened the last Sunday! The sister was walking around bitter in her spirit because of what had been said about her nearly twenty years ago.

I said to her, "If someone came into your house and immediately began to disrupt everything in your home, turning over furniture, breaking dishes, throwing food on the living room floor, would you allow this kind of behavior or ask them to leave?"

She said, "I would not have to ask them to leave. By the time they saw the look on my face and what I held in my hand, they would start running out of my house!"

I then asked, "Why, then, have you let what someone said about you so long ago come into your inner house and turn it upside down and inside out?"

She looked at me in amazement and said that from that day onward that there would be no room in her inner house for such negative intruders as the feeling she had been harboring in her heart. Learning to be still in the presence of the Almighty will translate into doing some interior house cleaning. Stillness unclutters the inner house, making it easier to find our quiet place in the secret closet of the soul.

Solitude activates the spark of heaven that lives in us that was placed there by the hand of our heavenly Father. We want to stir up this gift of God that was given to us the moment we encountered the living Christ. This is what the Apostle Paul was telling Timothy, his protégé in the gospel ministry, to do; that is, to stir up the gift of God that dwelled inside of Timothy. This stirring up, this activation of the holy spark, or what I have been calling the developing of our inner muscle, is one of the greatest joys that we can experience in life. Jesus wants to express Himself in us and through us. Each time we begin to let this spiritual desire in us take root through pondering upon a holy thought or favorite story in the Bible, it will begin to help us develop a powerful Christian walk. As we grow in our walk with the Lord, we will be abiding more and more in him, thereby producing much fruit.

You have been underestimating yourself for too long. The spirit of Christ has been tugging patiently at your soul to launch out into the deep and cast your net down for a great catch. His signals to go deeper are as quiet as a gentle whisper. This heavenly whisper may sound faint, but please don't confuse faintness with weakness, for the power of God's whisper contains breakthrough ability. Stillness will help you hear His whisper; solitude will empower you to walk in it. Glorious Christian living is the normal pattern of life for the child of God. To bring the glory out, we must go within. That is where the glory of the Lamb lives, moves, and has its being. Yes, in this silence we will shine. In this stillness, we will radiate. In the letter to the church at Ephesus, we are informed that we sit in the heavenly places in Christ. In order to possess your heavenly habitation, you must begin to do some sitting! Then you will learn that the highest in life is our natural home.

When I was a child, I loved to go down the street to my Grandmother Mary's house. She was a Chicago Cubs fan, and we would sit in front of the television cheering for our favorite player, Ernie Banks. As I sat in that living room with Grandmother Mary and enjoyed her company, she would give me treats that I did not have to ask for. I can still taste that hot buttered popcorn, ice cold pop, and many other delectable delights that are too numerous to mention. I enjoyed the fruit of being in her fellowship.

This is the same principle at work when we cultivate the joy of being in the presence of the Lord. We begin to partake of what our Lord possesses. These things of God, such as healing, prosperity, peace of mind, a deep sense of well-being, and creativity are given to us. In fact, Jesus said it is our heavenly Father's good pleasure to give us the kingdom. These gifts of God gradually become more and more a part of our lives as we grow in our reflection of the indwelling Christ Jesus. This increasing awareness of the indwelling Christ manifests in our thinking His thoughts, having His desires, and developing a Christian lifestyle. It is impossible to live with someone and not begin to take on some of the other person's personality.

The life that starts to live in the presence of Jesus will likewise be changed to resemble Him. The power of this union begins its great work far beyond our detection, deep within a place inside us that is reserved for God alone to reside and rule. It is that divine place in the child of God that the psalmist David described as the "dwelling of the Most High." Sitting in the Lord's sacred shadow is to become like a river that is connected to the ocean. The currents of the ocean flow powerfully, without interruption or effort, into that very river. You have entered into the overflow of the Lord, and you are granted what Emerson terms *a license of higher being*. This license to live as a citizen of heaven is our Christian birthright. Living the high life is the fruit of being born again.

Another term that Christ Jesus used in talking to His disciples about solitude and stillness involved going into one's "secret closet." We are instructed by Christ to enter into our secret closets frequently, and upon heeding the Savior's advice, the promise follows that our heavenly Father will then reward us openly. We will try and unfold what some of these rewards consist of later in our discussion, but let us say for now that the Apostle Paul tells us that we possess this treasure within our earthen vessels, that is, within our bodies. Now just because you do not see the treasure right there before your eyes does not mean that it does not exist. This treasure is something like the muscle that we have been talking about. It's just buried and hidden from our eyesight.

Millions of people overlook their treasure everyday even though they are walking around with it each second of their lives. Stillness in His presence, being in solitude beneath the shadow of the Almighty, is the inner map that leads us to the discovery of this divine treasure. Each time we quiet ourselves, we uncover more of the treasure that our Lord speaks of. What are you waiting for? Begin the process of entering your secret closet and become a treasure hunter!

A friend recently called to thank me for some advice that I had given him a number of years ago. The advice that I had given to him had become one of his favorite mottos. I had to confess to him that I had forgotten the conversation that he was calling to thank me for. That's when he said, "The conversation we had and the words you shared really stuck with me, for you told me one way to get the most out of every day was to do these three things, that is, attach at dawn, detach at noon, and unite at night. Then you explained to me what each thing meant, and it has helped me develop spiritually."

Let me also share with you the meaning behind attaching at dawn, detaching at noon, and uniting at night. The best way to start the day is to attach our minds in the morning to the word of God. Reading and meditating upon some uplifting verse in the scriptures sets the right tone for the beginning of your day. I know that your mornings are hectic, but if you would just set aside ten minutes in the morning to attach to the Christ through His Word, I guarantee that your mornings will become less chaotic. The next step is to repeat what you did in the morning during your attachment time somewhere around noon. By doing this exercise, you are detaching from the clutter that we so easily pick up as we go through the day at work or school. Finally, night is the time to unite with family and friends as well as repeating once again the reading and reflection upon the love of Jesus, that agape love that guided and kept us throughout the course of our day. This is one of my little exercises for growth that anyone can follow, and I hope it helps you as well.

CHAPTER TWO

Second Bite: The Mosaic Method of Slowing the Aging Process

My choice of Moses as a model for what I wish to talk about in this chapter is due to the fact that Moses went through a mid-life crisis and came out on top. If we examine his life, we soon discover that it reads like a rollercoaster ride. His birth involved death-defying maneuvers by a wise mother that saved his infant life. He was enrolled as a youth in the prestigious and highly exclusive private school of the pharaohs, which would ensure him of a very nice and comfortable quality of life. He made a tragic decision one day as an adult that resulted in seeing his early dreams go down the drain. He was forced to leave his professional career track of pharaoh-in-waiting at its apex and begin the process of starting his life all over again. The ramifications of what was revealed to him from this process shaped not only Moses' personal life, but profoundly molded the course of the people on this planet in such a way that we still feel the effects of the fruit of his encounter with God today. All this from his having a mid-life moment. Mid-life does not have to mean that half of your living is over and done with, that the remainder is full of refills of prescription bottles, appointments with the family physician, and daily battles with the bulge. Like Moses, mid-life can mean to climb our mountain and begin the entrance into our divine destiny.

If the Lord had not directed Moses to leave the career path that Moses was on as a protégé of Pharaoh, then Moses would not have lived to the ripe age that he did. The career trek that he was on was filled with headaches and heartburns, and Moses had no ready response to the environment that produced the pressure that would surely break down his body one day. Once he made the mid-life decision to change lanes and to elevate his way of thinking and living, the inner decision transformed his physical well-being. Did you ever notice that after encountering the presence of God at the burning bush, followed by frequent excursions climbing up Mount Sinai and being in intimate fellowship with our heavenly Father, that Moses never got sick? Illness cannot live around divine illumination. Encounters with the presence of God are spiritual tonic for the immune system. I firmly believe that fellowship with Jesus slows down our aging process.

As we consider the life of Moses, we observe that he travelled down two career tracks. His first one was in politics as an officer, a kind of pharaoh-in-waiting, inside of the government of Egypt. This initial path carried with it a lot of perks, good benefits, and a handsome salary. I know a little bit about political appointments, officers of the government and career paths, being that I have lived in our nation's capital for the better part of my life. Federal and city government appointments and jobs in Washington, DC, can be prized possessions. These same jobs, however, can become great sources of stress and anxiety the higher one climbs up the political ladder. Certainly Moses felt the tremendous strain of being one of the highest ranking officials in Egypt, and this pressure no doubt took its toll on his body. Have you ever noticed how most of our presidents begin to speed up the aging process once they have entered into their presidency? The weight of the Oval Office soon leaves its marks upon their countenance. Their political career is often marked with some type of physical breakdown before they leave their term of office. You don't have to run for political office to feel the debilitating effects of your job upon your health. Stress is no respecter of person, and most of today's jobs are stress producers. That's why professionals in the marketplace need to have access to this inner gym of the kingdom of God in their lives.

The second career that Moses had was as a blue-collar worker in the sheep industry. Moses was hired by his father-in-law Jethro to work as a shepherd. The work as a laborer in this field was tedious, filled with long hours and scorching conditions. Blue-collar work can give you the blues in a matter of seconds. Its damage to the body does not take long to be experienced. Going from a white-collar environment to a blue-collar environment was enough of a swing to knock Moses off his feet. Many people today have been forced like Moses to leave one type of career and enter into another. Many of us have discovered that we likewise are at a crossroad. Crossroads, however, are good when they can lead you to a more dynamic mindset and lifestyle.

It was at a crossroad in his life that Moses began to uncover the secret of slowing down the aging process. The journey began by Moses being introduced by God into a new dimension of living. This divine introduction occurred in the desert near a bush that burned but was not consumed by the fire, and the voice of the Lord saying to Moses , "Put off the shoes from off thy feet, for the place whereon thou standest is holy ground" (Exodus 3:5 ASV). The Lord uses crossroads in our careers and desert episodes in our lives to introduce us into a higher and greater way of thinking. Most of the time we have to be pinched out of our comfort zone before we begin to think of new possibilities developing within our lives. As long as the so-called guaranteed paycheck from our so-called steady job keeps coming every week or every two weeks, we are satisfied and complacent. This complacency is the norm of the majority of people despite the fact that our inner potential is greater than the weekly or bi-weekly paycheck that we have been receiving. When the Lord told Moses in the desert to remove his sandals, the Lord was telling him to start life from a higher point of view. Moses was told to remove the limitations that he had placed on his thinking.

Moses made his greatest discovery during one of the lowest points in his life. While he was at work among the sheep in the blistering heat of the desert, Moses stepped into a new awareness, a new dimension of thought and life. Moses entered into the kingdom of God gymnasium. This kingdom of God gym's primary purpose is to produce citizens of heaven. Now let's come to an understanding of what we mean when we say "heaven." Heaven is more than a physical location; heaven is first and foremost a divine and holy dimension. Dimension proceeds location. Dimension is about being born again, walking by faith and not by sight. Dimension involves life in the Holy Spirit and possessing what Paul the apostle called in one of his letters to the church the "mind of Christ Jesus." It means that we have begun to live life out of the overflow of our fellowship with our heavenly Father. If my daily walk is centered in this Christian dimension of life, then I begin to experience within my location the foretaste of the power of the new creation in Christ.

When those desert-like circumstances come into our lives, you can take great comfort in this divine truth: deserts are doorways that the Lord uses to enter us into the Jesus gym, that place of heavenly dimension. During my days as a young seminary student at Howard University in Washington, DC, I worked at a grocery store chain. One day the manager of the store told me to go into the meat freezer and clean it out. Little did I know that what was waiting for me inside that gigantic freezer was a block of ice the size of an iceberg! The freezer probably had not been cleaned since the invention of the automobile. As I stood there staring at the iceberg inside the meat freezer in total shock, the manager walked up to me with an ice pick in his hand and a devilish grin on his face. "You may need this ice pick." Needless to say, if I could have melted the ice by the temperature of my anger, the iceberg would have gone away in seconds. I wanted to quit on the spot and probably would have had it not been for the fact that I had a wife and a little baby at home, and we needed the money.

In a paradoxical kind of way, the meat freezer became my desert. Once the Lord shifted my focus from my anger to His presence, His Spirit told me to take a couple of whacks at the iceberg with the pick supplied by the boss. I prayed and let my prayer guide the ice pick. That's when Jesus revealed to me the power of focused prayer coupled with patient determination. I struck the iceberg three times. The Lord allowed me to hit that iceberg with the pick at the precise points where the ice would begin to crack. The mountain of ice crumbled before my eyes like a stack of cards! You should have seen the look on that manager's face when he came back about ten minutes later. I thanked him for the ice pick, took my time card, punched out, and headed toward school. Jesus allowed me to enter into His gym then guided me to the proper point of contact.

The biblical story of young David battling the giant Goliath comes to my mind. David used the lessons that the Lord had taught him while he sat in communion with the Good Shepherd and was able to defeat the giant. This youth who had a "heart stayed on God" picked up a stone and placed it in his slingshot. Guided by the aim of the Almighty, the little boy lodged the stone between the eyes of

Goliath with heavenly power, and the giant was last seen lying flat on his back.

The practice of dwelling within the presence of God has powerful effects on physical lives. It can produce the power to crumble an iceberg or defeat a giant. In the life of Moses, we see that it can also slow down the aging process. We are informed in the Old Testament book of Deuteronomy that when Moses passed from labor to reward and went home to be with the Lord, there was no weakness in his body, slowness in his step, or defect in his physical mobility. He was a great physical speci-men, even at the ripe age of 120 years old. "And Moses was a hundred and twenty years old when he died: his eye was not dim, nor his natural force abated" (Deuteronomy 34:7 ASV).

How was Moses able to accomplish this slow-ing down of aging process? After entering into this divine dimension of life called heaven, Moses con-tinued to nurture and cultivate this spiritual life that spilled over into his physical living by exercises of ascension and attachment. That is, Moses ascended frequently to places set aside for encountering the eternal and fellowshipping with our heavenly Father. Places like Mount Sinai, the Tent of the

Tabernacle, allowed Moses to deepen his spiritual awareness of the Almighty. One might say that Moses did intense ascension exercises on a weekly basis. However, he did hourly attachments to this new spiritual reality by praying throughout the day as well as mediating upon the Word and manifesting that manifestation in his daily walk. This gives us the spiritual formula for slowing down the aging process: attach hourly, ascend weekly.

What we ascend and attach to is our life in Christ, that is, our life increasingly reflects the Holy Spirit dwelling within us. God has given His children the divine capacity to connect with Him. It is our birthright, for we are made in His image and likeness. This image and likeness does not know anything about aging. The spiritual life resides outside of time and location, and the more we become at home with this heavenly inner life, the greater our rest within the indwelling presence of God, the less the effects of time (and aging is one of the direct results of time) dominate our lives. Now when I say ascend to God, I am not saying that we turn into a comic book character, raise our arms to the sky and shout, "Up, up, and away." By ascension I mean to return to the original intention that God had in His mind when He created us in His image and likeness.

Aging was never a part of the divine design for humanity. There is no mention of the process of aging until after the fall of man in Genesis. Before the fall, Adam and Eve were both forever young. That was due to their unbroken fellowship with God their Father. The nearer I stay to God, the newer my physical life becomes. Ascension is a prolonged inner focus upon heavenly things. Moses spent some long days and hours out in the desert in fellowship with God. During one stretch in his life, he spent forty days out in the desert in communion with the Lord and never got hungry or even thirsty. Moses was totally caught up in what Apostle Paul would later term "the spiritual body" in a letter that he wrote to the church at Corinth: "…there is a physical body, and there is a spiritual body…" (First Corinthians 15:44, NET).

The spiritual body lives outside of time and does not need things like food or water. It never wrinkles or aches; it remains forever young. Whenever you do any sort of prolonged ascension activity, you are making a major investment in the new life in Christ. I like to make my investments early in the day and late in the evening. I figure that if I can watch a one-hour television show or a two-hour football or basketball game (overtime games not included), then I can at least make the effort to give to Jesus the same amount of time in communion with Him. Of course, each should decide individually the amount of ascension time that works for you. The ultimate purpose of the practice of ascension into the presence of the Lord is not measured in minutes or hours but in mindset and consciousness.

Moses climbed the mountain to receive the Word of God and dwell in glory of the Lord that would end up transforming his way of thinking and living. The more Moses encountered God, the more the effects of this divine contact overflowed into his physical body. So we read in Exodus 34:29-30, "And it came to pass, when Moses came down from Mount Sinai with the two tables of testimony in his hand … Moses was not aware that the skin of his face shone … and when Aaron and the children of Israel saw Moses, behold the skin of his face shone … "(Exodus 34:29-30 ASV).

Let's examine what's happening here a little further, for it grants us a great glimpse into the outward effect of inner transformation. The time that Moses had spent with the Lord in ascension resulted in a physical transformation in his body. Although he was not aware of it, the face of Moses illuminated. There's a song that we sing in church that says, "This little light of mine, I'm going to let it shine. This little light of mine, I'm going to let it shine. Jesus gave it to me, and I'm going to let it shine. Let it shine, all the time, let it shine."

Moses became the living embodiment of this melody. His spiritual body had all the burners turned on, and the sparks from their inner flame manifested in his eighty-year-old face. The cause of this face-lift was not a prescription pill, but time sitting still in contemplation with God. The glow of God is waiting for you at the top of your mountain. At the top of this mountain is a higher way of thinking, which always leads to a better way of living. Moses received the Ten Commandments on his mountain, and these commandments are really divine directions on spiritual formation and uncovering the spiritual life.

The commandments were given for the purpose of countenance shining. When we allow our focus to be aimed toward ascension, it has a beneficial effect upon our mental health, immune system, physical well-being, and the healing process. I was talking to a young friend of mine yesterday, and during the course of our conversation he asked me if it depressed me to visit my sick members in the hospital as a part of my pastoral responsibilities. I replied, "Not at all," for I approach my ministry to those in the hospital as an opportunity to discover the spiritual body and its positive impact upon the physical body.

Let me share with you an example of what I'm referring to. One day I walked into a hospital room to see a member who had severe issues with her circulation, and the physician was talking about drastic surgery. When I entered her hospital room, she was staring at her swollen foot, the television was on with the volume turned up, and the look of deep depression was written all over her face. The first thing I did was to ask if the television could be turned off.

The next thing that I asked my member to do was to stop staring at her foot. I observed that her depression was linked to her staring at her present condition. "We are going to put our minds on some scripture and sing a song," I told her.

After about ten minutes of ascension concentration, she told me, "Pastor, you know I do feel better. It's like a chain has been broken inside of me."

Afterward, she stopped watching television as much and repeated our ascension exercise each day. Beforehand, the prescription that the doctor had given her had not produced the desired results, but after she shifted her focus to the spiritual life, the medication began doing its job. About a month later, I saw her walking into the worship service with a luminous smile .

Ascension is the art of learning how to live from the inside out. Living our lives from the inside out means not allowing the external conditions of life get behind our inner wheel and drive us off the road or stir us into a fit of road rage that leads to reckless lifestyles. This is not how we have been taught to live. We have been fooled into thinking and living just the opposite, that is, from the outside in. When you view life from the outside in, then you become like the disciples of Jesus who were on that boat being tossed around by angry waves and thought that the sea would become their watery cemetery. The storm on the outside infiltrated into their minds and hearts on the inside, and these disciples of Christ hit the panic button. Living life from the outside usually translates into people pushing panic buttons, the blood pressure being raised, and migraine headaches pounding a debilitating beat upon the head.

The alternative and healthier way is to live like Jesus, approach life from the inside out, and let the peace of God that dwells deep within us calm the storm that is raging outside of us. Jesus mastered the storm. He walked upon its waves. The violent winds obeyed His still, small voice, and the wind hushed like a scolded child sent into quiet time by the child's parents. Perhaps you're thinking that this lifestyle that stills the storm is beyond your capacity. Take a look at Peter. He was also able to overcome the storm. Jesus gave him a lesson on stepping through a storm and living life from the inside out. The lesson began for Peter when he was willing to step outside of the boat. As long as he was in the boat, he was a prisoner of limited understanding. Yet once he obeyed the call of Christ and left the boat of unbelief and a life chained to external conditions, moving instead toward his spiritual potential as a follower of Jesus, the storm no longer had its vice-grip hold upon him.

Leave your boat of limitation and move toward your spiritual possibility. Wisdom and understanding are the keys that open the door of ascension and communion with God. Peter stepping out of the boat and Moses climbing the mountain both represent how you and I can increase our knowledge of God and become closer with heaven. Our boundless capacity to receive is a reflection of God's divine desire to give unto us every good and perfect gift. The Lord's desire for us is perfect health. This perfect health is a byproduct of our progressive ascension into the awareness of the presence of the Lord and our steady attachment to the new life that flows from His presence. Don't become discouraged if your climb up your mountain of spiritual formation and understanding seems slow. Every step you take toward letting Christ our Lord dwell in you richly is a booster shot to your immune system.

In the Gospels, as far as I can tell, as long as the disciples followed Jesus, sickness did not strike their physical body. They were so close to the source of life and so connected to Christ that the overflow from that sacred connection spilled over into the maintenance of their health. The nearer one is to Christ, the newer he or she feels. This is the meaning of the word that Jesus spoke when He said, "Take my yoke upon you and learn of me. For my yoke is easy and my burden is light, and you shall find rest for your soul." The yoke stands for joining into Jesus, coupled with the Christ, wedded to the kingdom of heaven.

Whatever a person is plugged into, he becomes a part of. Association breeds assimilation. The Apostle Paul revealed the mysterious working of this assimilation when he said in his second letter to the Corinthian congregation, "But we all, with unveiled face beholding as in a mirror the glory of the Lord, are transformed into the same image from glory to glory, even as from the Lord" (2 Corinthians 3:18 ASV).

Ascension fosters assimilation. I recently did the pastoral installation service of one of my sons in the ministry. He was blessed by the Lord to be called to a loving and beautiful congregation in a wonderful part of the city. In our tradition, there is a part of the installation service where a charge is given to the newly called pastor. It was my pleasure to give him his charge, and I told this new pastor that the most important part of his ministry would involve two things, ascension and attachment. The pastorate can grow old and tiresome if there is no ascension time invested within it.

There is a mystery in the ministry of the Gospel of Jesus Christ that must be maintained or else the work becomes mundane. Being a coworker of Christ should recharge instead of crush you. Pastors, preachers, and ministers should be miniature heavens that walk the earth. Indeed, every child of God has been given the grace by our heavenly Father to become a reflection of the glory of God, according to the degree that he or she has put on the mind of Christ. This divine reflection is a step-by-step process. Moses did not run up his mountain; he climbed it one step at a time. Yet with each step that he took, the old Moses with the old way of seeing things was being replaced by a new Moses that began to see life from a higher point of view. This higher point of perception spilled over into a physical body that was full of health and vitality. Some people think and talk themselves into a state of sickness. The opposite can become your reality as well, you can enhance your well-being by embracing a spiritual thought and positive conversation.

Attachment must follow close behind ascension. As we encounter by way of ascension the image of

God that our Savior has renewed us unto, we must daily walk by way of attachment to this new creation. Think of attachment as a heavenly reminder of your celestial citizenship. Musicians are familiar with something that we call "muscle memory." Muscle memory means to correctly play a piece of music or properly hold a particular instrument based on repetition and practice. Utilizing the same principle, we also have a spiritual muscle memory. This spiritual muscle memory consists in acts of worship, scripture reading and reflection as well as prayer affirmations, just to name a few.

When we do these types of attachments throughout the day, we are reinforcing the spiritual encounter that happens during ascension time. The Apostle Paul was referring to spiritual attachment exercises during the course of our daily walk when he said to that we should speak to ourselves in psalms, hymns, and spiritual songs. Although we will dig a little deeper in the next chapter about spiritual formation and sound, it is enough to say for now that Paul is telling us to attach ourselves to what is good throughout the course of the day.

How do we know what is the good thought? The good thought has a certain kind of inner feeling. It's sort of like a basketball player who shoots a foul shot and has that inner feeling that the ball is going in the basket even before it leaves his or her fingertips. The attachment is always expressed as, Paul says, we are to speak it. As we speak it, we are reminded of it. This is vitally important because we may lose track of the ascension experience as the day progresses. Our days are so packed with busy schedules and work deadlines that the splendor of the ascension encounter soon fades away. Yet, acts of attachment bring back the shine.

When I was a little child, I started a hobby of collecting old pennies. I would perform scavenger hunts throughout the backyards of the homes of my neighbors and often I would find numerous types of coins. I found a few quarters, some dimes, and a whole lot of pennies. Most of the coins were in pretty unrecognizable condition; they had been outside so long that their shine was covered up by dirt and grime. I placed the coins that looked the worst in a jar in my room. One day as I was reading one of my comic books, I came across an advertisement offering a coin kit that promised to restore the coins' original shine. I saved up my allowance money and sent off for the coin kit.

The day that it arrived in the mail, I rushed into my room and took out the jar that held the dingy coins. Taking some coin cleaning solution out of the kit, I wiped the solution onto the coin. Within a matter of minutes I could see the original shine begin to return to the coin. Attachment that uses periodic prayer throughout the day, scripture affirmations and moments of silence, serve as the solution that restores the shine of our ascension. The spiritual shine has not gone anywhere; it's just covered up by all the confusion of daily life. Every beautiful thought that we think, any holy idea that we inwardly embrace, each truth of scripture that we attach our minds to—in other words, as we put on the mind of Christ—this attachment operates like a cleaning agent that recovers our brilliant shine.

When we combine ascension with attachment, we come up with a way to keep our attention on the presence of the indwelling Christ. Constant, unbroken, loving attention to the almighty Lord God was the original intent of God for humanity before the fall. In Christ, this divine intention is given new life. When our lives have recaptured the original focus of attention to the presence of heaven permeating our daily walk, then our course in life becomes easier. We think clearer when we are not tied up in knots, and our minds are free from clutter. Ascension and attachment leading to attention to the presence of Christ also translates into slowing down the aging process. When we practice this spiritual formation formula, our minds become tense-free and the inner man sits behind the steering wheel of our day-to-day lives.

This kind of stress-free living enhances our lives, making us healthier and happier. Happier people are healthier people. Spirituality-centered folk recover quicker from physical illness and emotional damage. The things that damage us physically are often related to the stress of modern life, fears of isolation, and insecurity over economic stability. These are symptoms of a sense of inner emptiness. The feeling of emptiness is a direct result of a lack of awareness of God's affirmative presence.

Jesus said that the kingdom of heaven is like a little child. Have you seen any children walking around with prescription bottles in their pockets? Do children race to a tiny tot happy hour to seek liquid consolation from a bartender? Of course not! Their little lives overflow with the inner awareness that a loving parent will provide. They need no external object to manufacture for them feelings of happiness and joy. Children can create this automatically based on their inner inventory of joyous thoughts and happy mindset.

When you live pressure-free, you do not have to search for a party in order to experience a good time. Good times belong to God. When He created the world, He called it good. Anyone who begins to see the world as God made it likewise becomes aware of its dynamic goodness, and he or she understands that having a good time is nothing more than a mindset. We see the world in this dynamic way by taking on more and more of the life of His Son. As we increase in our attention to the presence of Christ, we increase in Christ's likeness. This likeness to Jesus is rooted in our being made in the image of God. Ascend toward this image daily, detour and attach to it regularly, and it will become the focus of your attention.

Too many Christians have allowed the gift of attention to the presence of our heavenly Father to go on vacation. Our focus has become glued to illusions. What is an illusion? Anything that time can eat away or anything not rooted in the divine can qualify to be in the category of illusions of life.

One could say that Moses, prior to the burning bush encounter in the desert, was a person who hotly pursued the illusions of life. At the time that Moses was involved in them, they seemed to be the only things that mattered in life. His selfish political pursuits as the protégé of Pharaoh caused him to bask in the pleasures of a selfish lifestyle. When his career collapsed , Moses quickly saw that the things he had invested in were mere illusions. Yet Moses also represents those who begin to move beyond the illusionary grip of material life. When he turned toward the burning bush in the desert, it was symbolically a turning away from a surface-based lifestyle that was pulled here and there by an illusion like a puppet on a string to a life based on the inner dwelling of God.

I remember as a child, while playing over at my grandmother's house one day, picking up a piece of wax fruit from the basket in the dining room and biting into it only to discover that what I thought was a delicious red apple was in truth a piece of wax that had the look but nowhere near the taste of a real piece of fruit. Illusions look good, but they can't pass the test. When you bite into them, they leave you feeling empty and still hungry for the real thing.

In Exodus we are told that the Lord got Moses's attention by causing him to turn and see the burning bush. The Almighty has ways of getting our attention, sooner or later. These ways that the Almighty employs to get our attention are not sent to crush us but to cultivate our awareness of Jesus in our midst. Once this awareness happens, our whole world takes on a heavenly meaning and divine potential. We were called to launch out into the deep and cast our nets for a great catch.

I had some saintly godparents named Mr. and Mrs. Biggs. Each summer they would invite my brother and me to their summer cabin by the lake in the great state of Michigan. On one such trip, Mr. Biggs took us fishing on the shores of the lake. I looked into the water near my feet and saw some small fish swimming within close proximity. I let down my line near these small fish and caught a couple, but I noticed that Mr. Biggs had reeled in a catch that was five times the size of my fish. I asked him how he was able to catch such big fish. He replied, "If you want to catch big fish, you must leave the shore and cast out your line into the deep. We both have the same kind of fishing rods. Yours can go out into the deep waters just like mine if you only cast it out into deeper water ... " I did as I was instructed, and in a few minutes, I was hauling in a great catch.

We all have been given the same spiritual equipment by our heavenly Father to be able to launch our lives out into the great things of God. Don't say that Moses had something given to him that you or I do not have. Grace gives everyone the opportunity to travel beyond the surface and enter the kingdom of God. It is this deep communion with the Lord that contains the great blessings of God: His wisdom, healing, abundance, peace, rest, and prosperity reside in the deep. Are you ready to do some deep sea fishing? Jesus said that He would make us all fishermen. He was not just talking about telling sinners about the Gospel of Jesus Christ. Our Lord is also saying that His disciples are called to become dwellers in the deep waters of the kingdom of heaven. Jesus wants us to be demonstrators of a deep fellowship with God, manifesting unto the world the wonderful blessings that exist beyond the surface type of lifestyle. Our inner focus was fashioned by the Lord to be anchored in the awareness of heaven, the greater the awareness, the greater the demonstration and manifestation of the blessing.

Third Bite:
The Jesus Gym and Sound

The Bible spills over with examples of the importance and impact that uplifting and creative sound has on the child of God. Some folks even say that when God spoke and created the world, that this spoken word was in the form of a song. It is hard to argue against such an interpretation if we simply take a peep at the splendor of a starry night or the harmonious glory of the morning dawn, as both day and night reflect the glory of the Almighty. Sound in the form of song was given as a gift by God to humanity after the fall to help keep fresh within the consciousness of the collective race the memory of paradise and a higher state of human existence.

We are told in Genesis that Jubal was the first inventor of musical instruments. Jubal probably heard the gentle breeze on the morning wind as it blew among the tree limbs and stirred up the waves upon the waters, and this movement by nature spoke a soothing and calming tone to his soul. Trying to emulate this natural sound could have been the inspiration for Jubal to fashion the first instruments of sound, which in similar fashion helped to ease and bring peace to the soul as he played upon the first harp, lyre, or flute.

We are also told that Moses ascended the mountain named Sinai to commune with God as well as receive His commandments. Moses was led up the mountain by the sound of the trumpet. These holy and mysterious trumpet blasts became his heavenly guides that directed the man of God into the presence of the eternal. Remember, no other man was on Mount Sinai with Moses, for he was ordered by the Lord to come up alone. This music was heavenly. Its origin flowed from the brilliance of the kingdom of God, which was in full display upon the mountain.

The Lord uses sacred sounds to communicate to His children. Likewise, we are to use sacred sounds to harmonize our souls with Jesus. One of the best examples of this type of spiritual formation by the use of sound is the life of that little shepherd boy who became one of the great kings of Israel and models of the Christian faith. I speak of the journey of the seventh son of Jesse, better known unto us as David. Out of this spiritually centered life, the creativity of David leaped forward like a powerful waterfall. The outburst of the psalmist's creativity shook the foundation of the world and is still reverberating in the hearts of people around the world today.

This creativity that flows from the center of our spirituality is one of the pinnacle gifts that our Lord has given to His children. We live in a world that has a surplus of copycats and a shortage of creators. Christians are called to become instruments that our Lord can use to manifest the new creation. In fact, when we create, we are then walking the most closely with God. Our heavenly Father wants to see His children act like Him and walk in His creative footsteps. When we create, we are behaving like our heavenly Father's children.

Jesus instills this glorious gift of creativity within us. It is our divine birthright as believers in Him and citizens of the new creation in Christ. As free as the gift is, it does demand from us one essential thing if the creative stream of power is to flow through us, and that is that we must be in fellowship with the Savior. Where there is lack of fellowship with Christ, there is little of the flow of His creative energy travelling in us and through us. However, the child of God that is in pursuit of the heart of God will come to experience the creative life streaming forth from his life. As we walk in the power of the new creation and witness the flow of creativity emerging out of us, our perception of life starts to shift from the mundane to the divine. Our day-to-day life takes on a transcendent dimension. We become a people of holy expectations and high perceptions, Problems that once were seen as troublesome obstacles now become stepping stones to new opportunities and divine demonstrations of the activity of God in our lives. The closer we become to Christ, the more creativity gets a chance to run through us like a mighty river. Creative ability is the byproduct of a vibrant spirituality.

There are some folks who try and fit creativity into a small little box. Their definition of creativity is the only one they consider. True creativity can never be neatly categorized or placed into a nice little corner. Art and music are great examples of creative abilities, but they surely are not the only representations of it. We need not look any further than the great biblical figure of David to see how vast this gift of creativity truly is. This list of David's creative talents is utterly amazing. This seventh son of Jesse was not only a genius in the realm of musical ability, but he was also a statesman, general, soldier, politician, administrator, architect, builder of cities, business entrepreneur, prophet, and poet.

There is no one category that you can place David totally inside. His creativity explodes him out of every box. David shows us that there always exists a God-given creative response to our earthly needs. The question is not do we possess any creativity, but rather are we walking within our creative gift that the Lord has given unto us. Like David, God calls us to become more and more creative.

Nearly everyone has heard of the thrilling story of the battle between David, the little shepherd boy, and the giant called Goliath. But have you ever viewed this great story from the angle of God-inspired creativity, which the Lord had deposited within David? When David was sent by his father to see how his brothers and the army of the children of Israel were doing in their fight with Goliath, David was alarmed to discover that the battle against the giant was going so badly that the children of Israel were even afraid to approach Goliath. King Saul, who symbolizes the non-creative approach to life, had been using traditional and conventional methods in the war with the Philistine giant. Although these strategies employed by King Saul had proven to be unsuccessful Saul was so narrow in his focus and stubborn in his mind that he refused to try a different path to the giant problem. Saul was so stuck in his ways that when David volunteered to go to fight Goliath, Saul gave David the same failed weapons that the giant had already defeated.

David was polite and accepted the offer by Saul as a courteous gesture to the king, but David knew in his heart what he was going to do. "And Saul armed David with his armor, and he put a helmet of bronze on his head and he also armed him with a chest plate of armor. And David took his sword and tried to go forward but he could not. And David said to Saul, I cannot go forward with your armor for I have not tested them. So David took off Saul's armor" (1 Samuel 17:38-39).

True religion always is in process of re-evaluation. We must rid ourselves of the excess baggage that is bogging down our lives. I saw a sign the other day as I entered the airport. It said, "Carry-on baggage is now limited to one." That's what we should consider as we aim to take flight in our pilgrimage: we should limit the baggage that we carry with us. Saul could not conquer Goliath because he carried within him to much baggage, too much luggage, such as the luggage of a sense-dominated way of life, the baggage of a non-creative approach to life's challenges, and the carry-on suitcase of outdated traditions, useless forms and substance-less fashions. Saul's ultimate doom was his vice-like grip on a failed strategy that was the product of a disconnected and dormant spiritual life.

Putting his lifestyle another way, Saul had a diminishing focus and decreasing devotion to the presence of the Lord in his life. That is, his lack of focus led to failure to fellowship with our heavenly Father. When you have a decreased focus alongside a diminished fellowship, the end result will always be a falling away from the path and pursuit of our divine purpose. The first sin committed upon the earth was the product of a decreased focus, one that Adam and Eve permitted to become dominant in their thoughts so much so until Satan was able to distract them from their divine heritage and replace it with a willful disobedience that was full of pride and arrogance.

The right spiritual focus is the powerful force in this life that will defeat Goliath every time. Goliath, as a reminder for us, represents the daily obsta-cles and constant challenges that we all encounter no matter our level of education, amount of economic attainment, or social status . Everybody has a Goliath to deal with. We each come across difficulties that we have never seen before. These unforeseen difficulties and unanticipated challenges demand the anointed approach of a focus that is fresh from the presence of the Holy Spirit.

I remember growing up in the Midwest in a wonderful city called Fort Wayne, Indiana. Many of the lovely folks who lived in my community were employed in the automotive and truck factories. These huge factories were the vehicles in the fifties and sixties that propelled many residents of Fort Wayne into the middle-class . In those days, the salaries and benefits offered to the workers easily equaled that of college graduates. Some of my friends and former high school classmates, instead of going to college, made the decision to stay at home, work in the factory, and raise a family in Fort Wayne. The lure of beautiful homes in the suburbs and a six-figure salary took hold of their heart.

What they did not foresee was the Goliath called "technology" and the global manufacturing industry that completely transfigured the factory industry in Fort Wayne and utterly wiped out the promise of a fat paycheck on Friday, along with a forty year career in the automotive machine factory industry. The high school graduates of the seventies who may have dreamed of following in their father's footsteps soon found out that the suit of the former days would not work during our time. The form of life that our fathers knew that provided a terrific means to feed their families in Fort Wayne vanished with the appearance of the computer chip. We had to take on a new mindset, one that many of our parents with their blue-collar frame of reference to the workforce never had to fully consider. The only way that we would be able to successfully confront this new challenge would be through the process of us taking off the old way of thinking and putting on a new mindset.

When you allow your quiet time to spark your creativity into a flame, you then break out of the herd-like crowd and begin to perceive new paths. Meditation in the presence of the Lord baptizes and sanctifies the imagination. It was the sanctified imagination of the young shepherd boy David that conceived a plan to beat Goliath. The same holds true in our day-to-day contests. Once we break out the herd, the Holy Ghost can give us the winning game plan. The Apostle Paul is alluding to this when he wrote, "Do not be conformed to this present world, but be transformed by the renewing of your mind, so that you may test and approve what is the will of God, what is good and well-pleasing and perfect" (Romans 12:2, ASV).

Re-examine your mindset. Reconsider your consciousness. Sooner or later you will awaken to the reality that Saul's suit must be removed if forward progress in life is to be made. Don't be fooled into thinking that the economic recession affects the spiritual imagination index. There is no shortage of imagination with the economy of the kingdom of heaven. The issue is not about a shortage of supply, but rather the need to launch out past the shallow waters of surface religiosity into fellowship with the spirit of Christ. Let your soul swim in the ocean of God. Get your feet wet in the fellowship with our heavenly Father.

Whatever you spend your time thinking of and being around, you eventually become similar with. The company that we keep, both our inward thoughts and outward associations, prove to shape and mold us. Jesus said that wherever our treasure is, there will our heart be also. As soon as we start to treasure the presence of God, permitting Christ to have His way in our thoughts and actions, His unapproachable light becomes reflected in us, and His resources of creativity, insight, and wisdom become ours to possess. David treasured being in the presence of the Lord, and because he did, his creativity increased.

One of the things that we know David did to increase the gift of creativity was to play sacred music and sing praises unto the Lord. In fact, the prayer life of David and his music can not be separated. It is utterly impossible not to notice the dominant role that music played throughout the course of his life. It was his skillful harp-playing that first caught the attention of King Saul and caused David to become a part of Saul's administration. As the pressure mounted in the monarch's life, Saul discovered that the sounds flowing from the harp of David put his stormy mind and spirit at ease: "And it came to pass, when the evil spirit from God was upon Saul, that David took the harp and with his hand: so Saul was refreshed and was well, and the evil spirit departed from him" (First Samuel 16:23, ASV).

The Lord had revealed to David in his youth the power of anointed sounds and sacred praise unto the Lord God of heaven and earth. David created a heavenly songbook called the Psalms. David composed and played heavenly hymns. His understanding of heaven is well worth our attention. The psalmist understood heaven as being much more than a physical location but also a holy dimension. David realizes that the heavenly dimension produces the heavenly location. He got this insight as he pondered the book of beginnings called Genesis. It was there where David saw the heavenly, spiritual dimension forming, creating, and producing all the beautiful and wonderful physical and material things upon the earth.

Is this not what our Savior did when Jesus spoke to the fierce wind that frightened the disciples into a state panic as their boat was overtaken by a sudden storm? Jesus spoke the word of peace to the storm: "But as they sailed, he fell asleep; and there came down a storm of wind on the lake; and the boat began to fill with water, and they were in jeopardy. And he himself was in the stern, asleep on the cushion; and they awoke him, and say unto him, Teacher; carest thou not that we perish? And he awoke, and rebuked the wind, and said unto the sea, Peace be still. And the wind ceased, and there was a great calm" (Mark 4:37-39, ASV).

The word spoken by Christ calmed the wind and silenced the storm. There is more power in a creative, heaven-connected word or song than in any storm that may come our way. Joyful sounds are invigorating to the soul. It is hard to sing a happy melody and be sad at the same time. When Adam and Eve long ago lost the privilege of paradise and were expelled from the Garden of Eden, this tragic expulsion was not merely physical, but more significantly, it was mental. Their thoughts no longer cherished the loving presence of the Lord. Their minds moved away from being anchored in God. They began to inwardly fade away from the embrace of the divine and soon ceased to enjoy the dominant thought of dwelling in the presence of the Almighty.

Sin is sneaky. It enters the mind and thought first and plants a seed of disconnection that is meant to separate us from ever thinking about the Lord. After the seed is planted and if allowed to take root, it will choke our spiritual life until we become numb to the center and source of our existence, Jesus Christ.

Yet the book of Genesis also begins to give us a peep on how the Lord would begin to start the process of a return unto Him. One of the descendants of Adam and Eve, by the name of Jubal, became the father of those who pioneered sound of praise and sacred melodies: "... and his brother's name was Jubal; he was the father of all those playing the harp and organ" (Genesis 4:21, Modern King James Version of the Bible). Jubal, of whom the psalmist David was surely a musical heir, brought back the awareness of being found in our Lord's presence. Along with this return in thought back to the Lord came also the returned embrace of paradise. After the fall of humanity, people began to struggle for survival. The grace of God provided the gift unto Jubal to play his stringed instrument and thus supply the sacred sound that gave a heavenly reminder for those struggling to exist that they were not battling alone. The holy sound sent the signal to the listener that the Lord was always present, even in the midst of their problems.

We could say that Jubal was one of the earliest reflectors of the grace of God. His gift was to bring music into the world. The musical chords of Jubal carried a celestial tune. They uplifted the spirit beyond the flesh-centered, material-dominated lifestyle and pointed to the divine possibilities of a new paradise, a new heaven, and a new earth. Sacred sound always contains a heavenly scent that only the soul can detect. With this spiritual detection comes the aspiration for ascension into the shadow of the Almighty. The psalmist mentions a few dividends of those who start to dwell beneath this shadow of the Almighty: "He that dwelleth in the secret place of the Most High shall abide under the shadow of the Almighty. I will say of the Lord, He is my refuge and fortress; My God in whom I trust. For he will deliver thee from the deadly pestilence. He will cover thee with his pinions and under his wings shalt thou trust … thou shalt not be afraid for the terror by night, nor for the arrow that flieth by day … He will give his angels charge over thee, to keep thee in all thy ways … "(Psalm 91:1-12).

Look at these tremendous dividends of dwelling in the shadow of the Almighty: a refuge and fortress, security, deliverance and direction. These are all things that we crave in our society, a society that is appearing more and more fragile and overwhelming to many people. People are searching for change and a new world, something that the psalmist reveals how to produce. The power of a new creation with unlimited potential is ours by birthright as born-again citizens of the kingdom of Christ. Our call is to help repair the rupture in a fractured world. Thus David, as he played upon his harp, soothed the ruptured soul of King Saul. His sacred brooding led Saul on the path toward restoration.

That's what happens when we reconnect with Christ Jesus and begin to become harmonized with the kingdom of heaven: the Lord does repair work within us, resulting in a progression in our daily living. The collapse of King Saul was due to a disconnect in his life. This inward disconnection led to Saul experiencing emotional wear and tear which stripped his life. His position as King of Israel placed him within a pressure cooker, and Saul could not control the anger or pessimism in his life until it all reached unto a boiling point which led to his breakdown.

Many of the occupations we are pursuing in life—our work, careers, family, and schools—have the potential to bring us to a boiling point . Modern life can be nerve-wrecking. Yet our peace of mind and our healing is well within our reach. This kingdom of heaven within us is what David understood as the true temple of the Lord.

This understanding of the temple is quite different from what the casual church attendee may know as the "temple." David was aware that the sacred scriptures placed a spotlight on two temples, an inner one and an outer one. Most people place the majority of their attention on the outer, physical temple. That is, the physical building where people can physically go for worship is the only conception that far too many of the masses possess. When your only conception of the temple is the outer one, you're existing below your birthright as a child of God.

I have been privileged to serve as Senior Pastor of churches in two states, and one thing that they don't teach you in seminary is the building maintenance and repair cost. The physical temple is always in need of repair work and building upkeep. But the symbol for the physical building called the church, or temple, should always lead us to the reality of the inner temple, no matter how much work needs to be done on the physical building facility. The true purpose of the church-building is to give us a holy reminder that we are the true temple of the Lord. The outer temple is the one made by human hands, but the inner temple is made by the hand of the Lord.

Entering into the Jesus Gym is all about beginning to develop this new understanding of what the temple is, of what the church is. Jesus has also granted us a free, lifelong membership in His gym. It does not yet appear what you will become as you begin your workout with the Lord as your guide. Yet, rest assured, you shall become like Him.

ENDNOTES

1   The Portable Emerson: edited by Carl Bode in collaboration with Malcolm Cowley, Penguin Books

2   Meister Eckhart: A Modern Translation, Raymond Bernard Blakney, Harper Perennial Publishers